W9-AOE-902

Date: 9/18/12

**J 363.728 JAM
James, Lincoln.
Where does the garbage go? /**

Everyday Mysteries

Where Does the Garbage Go?

By Lincoln James

Gareth Stevens
Publishing

Please visit our website, www.garethstevens.com. For a free color catalog of all our high-quality books, call toll free 1-800-542-2595 or fax 1-877-542-2596.

Library of Congress Cataloging-in-Publication Data

James, Lincoln.
Where does the garbage go? / Lincoln James.
    p. cm. — (Everyday mysteries)
Includes index.
ISBN 978-1-4339-6327-8 (pbk.)
ISBN 978-1-4339-6328-5 (6-pack)
ISBN 978-1-4339-6325-4 (library binding)
1. Refuse and refuse disposal—Juvenile literature. 2. Recycling (Waste, etc.)—Juvenile literature. I. Title.
TD792.J36 2012
363.72'82—dc23

2011024744

First Edition

Published in 2012 by
Gareth Stevens Publishing
111 East 14th Street, Suite 349
New York, NY 10003

Copyright © 2012 Gareth Stevens Publishing

Designer: Katelyn E. Reynolds
Editor: Greg Roza

Photo credits: Cover, pp. 1, 7, 13, 17, 21 (garbage cans, bulldozer, recycling bins, garbage pile), (pp. 3–24 background and graphics) Shutterstock.com; p. 5 Denis Felix/Taxi/Getty Images; pp. 9, 21 (garbage truck) iStockphoto.com; p. 11 Justin Sullivan/Getty Images; p. 15 Digital Vision/Thinkstock; p. 19 iStockphoto/Thinkstock.

Printed in the United States of America

CPSIA compliance information: Batch #CW12GS: For further information contact Gareth Stevens, New York, New York at 1-800-542-2595.

Contents

Boldface words appear in the glossary.

Take Out the Trash!

Homes, schools, and businesses make a lot of garbage. That includes banana peels, paper towels, soup cans, and many other things. Where does all that garbage go after we put it by the street? Let's find out!

Working with Garbage

The people who take the garbage away from our homes are called **sanitation** workers. They have to get up early every day. They also have to be strong and healthy. It's hard to lift garbage all day long!

Garbage Trucks

Sanitation workers put garbage into big trucks. Many garbage trucks have moving walls inside them. These walls crush the garbage so it doesn't take up as much space. That way, the workers can fit a lot more garbage into the truck!

At the Station

After garbage trucks are full, sanitation workers drive them to **transfer** stations. The garbage is sorted and loaded onto larger trucks. Some is loaded onto trains or boats. It's taken to different places based on the type of garbage.

10

Sorting Garbage

At transfer stations, some types of garbage are removed because they're harmful to the **environment**. These include car batteries, tires, and refrigerators. Some types of garbage, such as plastics, are taken out because they can be **recycled**.

13

What Are Landfills?

More than half the garbage collected in the United States ends up in landfills. A giant hole is dug in the ground. Garbage is placed into the hole and covered with soil. When the hole is filled, the landfill is closed.

Land Reuse

Landfills are safer for the environment than they once were. They're placed where they can't harm wildlife and water supplies. Some closed landfills are turned into places where animals can live. Others are turned into parks or golf courses.

Garbage Power!

Some power plants burn garbage to make **energy**. These plants are called waste-to-energy plants. They help get rid of garbage. Closed landfills give off a gas called methane. This gas can be used to make energy, too.

Reduce, Recycle, Reuse

We can **reduce** the amount of garbage we put in landfills. Recycle plastic bottles, metal cans, and paper. Reuse plastic bags instead of throwing them away. Some people save leftover food and bits of cut grass to make **compost** for their gardens.

That's Where Garbage Goes!

1. Sanitation workers put garbage into a truck.

2. The truck takes garbage to a transfer station.

3. Some garbage is burned to make energy.

4. Some garbage is recycled.

5. Most garbage goes to a landfill.

RECYCLING CENTER

21

Glossary

compost: matter made from rotten food and cut grass. It's added to soil to make it better.

energy: power used to do work

environment: the natural world

recycle: to treat something so it can be used again instead of throwing it away

reduce: to cut down on the amount of something

sanitation: having to do with actions taken for health and cleanliness

transfer: having to do with moving something from one place to another

For More Information

Books

Green, Jen. *Garbage and Litter*. New York, NY: PowerKids Press, 2010.

LeBoutillier, Nate. *A Day in the Life of a Garbage Collector*. Mankato, MN: Capstone Press, 2005.

Nelson, Sara E. *Let's Reduce Garbage!* Mankato, MN: Capstone Press, 2007.

Websites

Beneficial Land Reuse
www.thinkgreen.com/beneficial-land-reuse
Find out how old landfills have been made into parks and land for wildlife.

Reduce, Reuse, and Recycle
kids.niehs.nih.gov/recycle.htm
Learn more about recycling and reducing the amount of garbage you make.

Index